Meditations on
saving our
home, Planet
Earth.

How anyone can
step up and do
their small part
in making the
world a better
place.

by Todd
Ermantrout

Dedicated to
Lalla

Chapter 1: The Power of Meditation

When I first began meditating, it seemed peculiar to me. Taking time to "quiet my mind". In the beginning, it did feel relaxing, but I would often fall asleep. With so many things to do in the real world, it seemed a waste of time to nod off and nap on purpose.

After a short time however, I began to feel as though my mind began to "wake up" and show signs of life. I

began to have
deep thoughts
and problem
solve. I was then
starting to plan
and integrate my
thoughts in more
meaningful
ways.

I also began to
focus on what is
truly important in
life...the real
meaning of it all.
In the end, when
you are
reflecting back
on your life, did
you truly do the
important things
that mattered...?
Or did you
escape into
various
distractions to
avoid living
authentically?

I propose that
you give
meditation a try

if you haven't
already.   I
think you will be
pleasantly
surprised and
find that your
valuable time
was spent
wisely.

<u>Action 1</u>: Start
meditating 10
minutes per day.
Then
incrementally
increase the
time as you start
to reap the
rewards.

Chapter 2:
"It is what it is"

With the state of
the world, it is
easy to put your
hands up and
tell yourself: "It
is what it is".

What can you
do to change
things? Even if
you made one
small change,
like starting to
recycle your
garbage, what
real difference
will this make in
the large scale
of things?

This view I've
found is
common, so
people continue
to go about their
lives without
giving any more
thought to it.

What if,
however, you
made small
consistent
changes?
Wouldn't such
changes make
your carbon
footprint just that
much smaller?
Think about it.

I propose that
making small
and consistent
changes will add
up over time.
Especially if
your friends and
family become
motivated to
take up your
pursuit.

In essence, if
enough of us
see the true
state of things
and follow suit,
there will be
"snowball effect"
which could

have dramatic
consequences
for all.

The timeframe
scientists are
giving us is that
we must act
soon, we must
begin today!

Action 2: take
one small step
to lower your
carbon footprint
today. No matter
how small it
seems. No
ideas...? Start
with recycling.

Chapter 3:
Global Warming

As much of the
world uses
carbon based
fuel to run the
world, how can
we convince the
multi-national
corporations and
the world
governments
that this is
urgent and must
be acted upon
right now?

It is no secret
that multi-
national
corporations are
motivated by the
profit motive,
and the world
governments
are often reliant
on private
investments in
the economy
and taxes. Also

take into account, that if we stopped using fossil fuel abruptly, much of the economy would shut down. Most of our electricity is produced through carbon based sources, so in essence, we would have an energy crisis.

To address this massive worldwide dilemma, we will need to tackle it step by step. We would have to take fuel based sources that supply the energy offline step-by-step. Simultaneously, we would need to replace our energy

production
mechanisms
with non-carbon
or "green"
solutions. So it
clear, we will
need to
construct the
infrastructure for
green
technology and
ensure it is
working
correctly, before
taking the
carbon based
systems offline
for good.

Imagine how
great that would
be...clean
energy with no
added
environmental
pollutants
entering the
atmosphere.

<u>Action 3</u>: Create a step-by-step plan at the grass-roots level changes promoting green energy solutions with families and then small businesses. As an electorate, we woul also lobby the Government for green rebate programs and for building the infrastructure for green energy industries. Then we would start building these industries from the ground up. Once online, let's shut off the Carbon systems one-by-one.

Chapter 4:
Measuring and
Reporting
Global Warming

Scientists
continue
measuring the
ozone layer,
polar ice caps,
etc., to give us
their best
educated
guesses on the
current state of
Global Warming.
These reports
should be made
an Agenda item
at every meeting
with all
Governments
and boardroom
meetings at
multi-national
Corporations.
These reports
should be
documented,
studied, and

integrated into
Governmental
and Corporate
cultures.

The information
should also be
publicly
available to the
masses. Groups
and movements
should be
formed in all
communities to
come up with
Regional and
Local plans
(small scale) for
the transition to
green energy.
Updates of
these groups
would be posted
online, so ideas
can be shared
and improved
upon.

This reporting
will motivate
everyone to be
persistent and

determined in turning things around for everyone inhabiting this planet.

If the Objective goal of life is to propogate the species, we must take care of this planet to ensure our children have a healthy place to live.

Action 4: Receive regular reports on the state of Global Warming. This will keep motivating us to address it.

Chapter 5: Love of the Automobile

We all need to get around. However, we must think of ways using "clean or green energy" in getting us from Point A to B.

We especially love having the freedom of having our own automobiles. This is a love affair I can understand.

When listening to Elon Musk of Tesla, I became inspired by what his vision was.

Imagine a "clean or green energy" vehicle that

looked stylish
and comfortable,
and was able to
deliver 0 to 60
miles per hour in
a decent time?
This may be a
long way off;
however, at
least Elon is one
pioneer who is
working on
delivering a
healthy
alternative for
the planet while
satisfying our
"need for
speed".

Dare I say,
"clean or green
energy" transit
systems? The
thought to me
was daunting,
as I used to take
public transit
each and every
day to
University.
Would you take

public transit if it operated on "clean energy"? Remember, one little change will lower your carbon footprint.

<u>Action 5</u>: Look into "clean and green energy" vehicles, such as the Tesla. Consider Public Transport if it uses "clean or green energy"

Chapter 6:
Extinction of
Species

It is daunting to
think of all the
pollutants
poured in the
oceans of the
world. I've seen
many photos of
dead or dying
sea creatures
that are exposed
to them. Not to
mention the
possible
detrimental
effects that may
be passed on to
their offspring.

Although we as
a species act as
if we own and
control this
planet, we are
just one species
of many.

Considering that
we as a species
have the most

impact on Earth, we must take responsibility and make it a better place than the way we found it. We must consider cleaning up the oceans. Ocean nations should consider charging garbage dumpers huge fines or imprisonment if they are caught, and require them to clean up their mess and restore the ocean they effected.

Sea life should also be monitored in numbers, as well as noting any genetic anomalies that are observed.

We should also focus on problem areas in the oceans, and deal directly with those governments showing a lack of care. Educate them on what repercussions of their actions are, and then encourage them to clean up the ocean that surrounds them.

Action 6: Inspect sea life and identify problematic ocean areas. Encourage governments to punish companies or individuals who dump in the

ocean. Lastly,
clean up the
oceans by
whatever
technologies we
have at our
disposal.

Chapter 7: Polar
Ice Caps

I'm aware that
the Polar Ice
Caps are being
measured. Last I
was informed,
they are melting
at an alarming
rate. Chris
Hedges,
Pullitizer Prize
Winner, recently
stated from his
research on the
matter, that the
situation is dire
and we may
only have 10
years left before
they melt away.
He then
mentioned that
the Planet
Venus used to
have water, but
enviromental
changes caused
the water to
evaporate and
now the planet

is 800 Degrees
Celsius. Imagine
if the same were
to happen on
Planet Earth?

If the overall
temperature on
Earth rises just 2
degrees on
average, the
Polar Ice Caps
will melt away
and Global
Warming will
begin on a
massive level.

As all ecological
systems are
interrelated, a
breakdown of
one system will
start a domino
effect. All
systems will be
in jeopardy.

Action 7:
Monitor state of
Polar Ice Caps
and the overall
rise in the

temperature of
the Earth. Keep
the masses
informed so that
they are
motivated to
persist in solving
this impending
crisis.

Chapter 8: Reaching out to your Political Base

As a single voter in a democratic nation, you have the right to contact your elected official and ask for action. If they vote against Environment measures, you may not vote for them in the future, right?

We must explore local and regional movements that we may join. With like minds, you can work as a group in making real change possible.

There is
strength in
numbers.
Governments
and
Corporations
also tend to
notice groups
and will
sometimes work
with them. No
matter, we must
try and connect
with them so
real progress is
made.

Once a shift in
the Zeitgeist
occurs regarding
Global Warming,
the masses will
being to look the
same way and
work towards
common goals.
We must work
stridently until
this day comes.
With patience,
hard work and
determination,

we can get
there. Believe it.

<u>Action 8</u>:
Connect with
your Politicians,
Corporations
and local
Environmental
Movements to
change the
current Zeitgeist.
When we are all
on the same
page, change
will happen
much more
quickly. Maybe it
will give us
enough time to
turn things
around!

Chapter 9: Living Busy Lives

Many of us live very busy lives. We really don't have time to lobby Government, connect with Corporations, or join Environmental movements.

We must make an effort to make time! As time is running short my friends...

To start, consider using Social Media to get into the hearts and minds of your family, friends, and others.

Do your best to

use facts and gentle persuasion to get your points across. Avoid being overbearing, as this will often backfire.

Also, try speaking with your friends and families about the true state of affairs. Give the facts as you know them and resources where they can check it out for themselves. Lead by example. Show them the small steps you have taken to reduce your carbon footprint and encourage them to give it a try. If they also convince others, this will have a trickle effect.

Action 9: If time is limited, start with Social Media. Give the facts and gently persuade. Also speak with friends and family. Lead by example and challenge them to try living "clean".

Chapter 10:
Final
Meditations

I wrote this
because I care
about the planet.
I want my
children to have
a healthy planet
to live on when
I'm long gone.
The human
species is
remarkable.
Look at what we
accomplished in
the last 100
years. It's
amazing!

With that same
determination,
hard work and
intelligence, I
am confident
that if we all
work together,
we can

overcome this massive challenge for humankind's sake.

My hope is that each one of us, starts with small steps to lower our carbon footprints. This is a start - no matter how small.

Let's save the home we love and preserve it for future generations...!

<u>Action 10</u>: Start with small steps to lower your carbon footprint. Constantly

remind yourself
about why you
are doing this
and why it is the
right thing to do.

www.ingramcontent.com/pod-product-compliance
Lightning Source LLC
Chambersburg PA
CBHW051139250726
48655CB00007B/3149